Levers

By Elsie Nelley

Contents

T0342771

How Levers Work

Levers are simple machines that people use to help them move loads easily.

A lever is usually a strong bar that turns on a pivot called a fulcrum. When force or effort is applied to the lever by pushing or pulling, the bar turns at the fulcrum and the load moves.

Many levers work because the fulcrum lies between the force and the load.

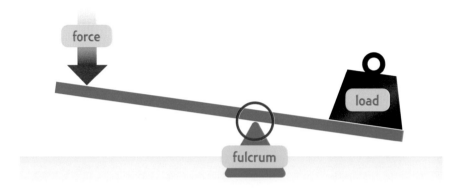

For example, the handles and blades of a pair of scissors are joined at the fulcrum. When force is applied to the handles, the blades move together and apart in a cutting action.

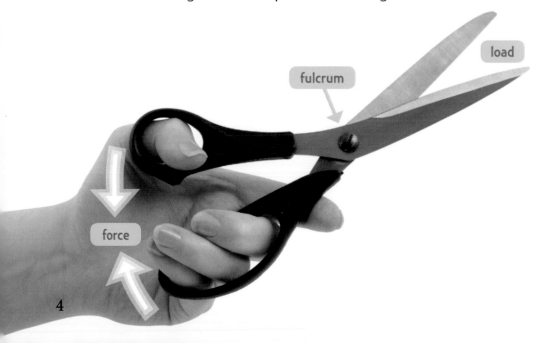

If paper is placed near the ends of the blades, only little cuts are made.

If the paper is placed closer to the fulcrum, long cuts are made. This makes the job of cutting easier because the force is magnified the closer an object is to the fulcrum.

Some levers work because the load lies between the force and the fulcrum.

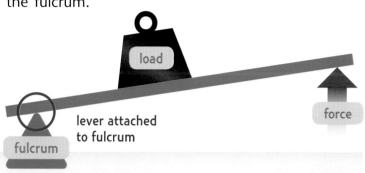

For example, when the handles of a loaded wheelbarrow are pulled upwards, the wheelbarrow can be lifted with a minimum amount of force. The wheel is the fulcrum and the load is between the handles and the wheel.

However, the wheelbarrow is only able to move heavy loads from one place to another because the wheel is also a simple machine. Levers are often attached to other machines to make them work more efficiently.

a water pump

A fishing rod and a broom are levers that work when force is applied between the fulcrum and the load.

A broom is held in two places. The fulcrum is the hand that supports the top of the handle. The other hand grips the handle further down. It is this hand that applies the force that moves the broom across the ground.

Levers have a minimal number of moving parts. This is why they are called "simple machines".

a stapler

pruning shears

a shovel

a hammer

The Crowbar

The crowbar is a metal tool designed to be used as a lever.

Large boulders and slabs of concrete can be moved using a crowbar. Construction workers use different types of crowbars to dislodge old roofing materials, pry objects apart, take out rotted beams and remove nails.

Crowbars can be used to increase force and leverage, or lifting movement. When applying force at one end of a crowbar, movement is created under the load. This happens because the force of pushing or pulling at one end of the crowbar changes into a powerful lifting movement at the other end.

Crowbars are most often made from steel. This material is strong and resistant to bending, except under severe force. Some crowbars are made from titanium, which is a light metal. Titanium crowbars are not as heavy as solid steel crowbars. This makes them the preferred tool on some construction sites even though they are more expensive to purchase.

Most hardware stores sell crowbars. They come in a number of different sizes and weights depending upon how the tool is to be used. Many workers involved with building, demolition and roofing keep more than one crowbar in their toolkit. This ensures they always have the right crowbar for a particular job.

There are several variations of crowbars.

The large crowbar is a long straight steel bar. One end is slightly curved with a chisel shape. The other end is often pointed.

Smaller crowbars have one large curved end. This end is forked so that it can be used to grip and pull out nails or other small objects. The other end is shaped like a chisel and can be forced between objects to move them.

The crowbar is not a new tool. Variations of this type of lever have been used for thousands of years.

The ancient Egyptians used levers to help lift stone blocks to build the pyramids.